BECOMING YOUR
CAT'S
BEST FRIEND

BECOMING YOUR CAT'S BEST FRIEND

BY BILL GUTMAN

ILLUSTRATED BY
ANNE CANEVARI GREEN

Pet Friends
The Millbrook Press
Brookfield, Connecticut

Published by The Millbrook Press, Inc.
2 Old New Milford Road
Brookfield, Connecticut 06804

Printed in the United States of America
5 4 3 2 1

Library of Congress Cataloging-in-Publication Data
Gutman, Bill.
Becoming your cat's best friend/by Bill Gutman:
illustrated by Anne Canevari Green.
p.   cm.—(Pet friends)
Summary: Questions and answers explain why cats knead
with their claws, what a cat's twitching tail means,
and other mysteries of the feline world.
ISBN 0-7613-0200-X (lib. bdg.)
1. Cats—Juvenile literature.   2. Cats—Behavior—Juvenile
literature.   [1. Cats—Miscellanea.   2. Pets—Miscellanea.
3. Questions and answers.]   I. Green, Anne Canevari, ill.
II. Title.   III. Series: Gutman, Bill. Pet friends.
SF445.7.G87   1997
636.8—dc20   96-31368   CIP   AC

The author would like to thank

Dr. Alan Peterson, DVM,

*of Community Animal Hospital
in Poughkeepsie, New York,
for his careful reading of
the manuscript and his many
helpful comments and suggestions.*

UNDERSTANDING YOUR PETS

Animals have always played a major role in people's lives. In earlier days, animals did a great deal of work. Oxen pulled the plows that tilled the fields. Horses provided transportation. Dogs were used to guard people and herds of cattle or flocks of sheep. Wherever there were people, there were usually animals, too.

Today, animals are still a big part of many people's lives. Some still work. Others are kept in zoos or on game farms. And countless millions of animals are simply family pets.

There is much more to pet care than feeding and housing. Whether you have a dog, a cat, a bird, tropical fish, a hamster, a gerbil, a guinea pig, or even a horse or pony, you owe it to that animal to learn all you can about it. Obviously, animals can't tell you their feelings. You have to guess what they are thinking and feeling by the way they are acting—by their sounds, their movements, and by changes in their behavior.

This is very important if you want to have a happy, healthy pet that will live out its natural life span. The Pet Friends series will not only discuss basic animal care. It will also strive to show what your pet thinks and feels as it lives its life with you.

YOUR PET CAT

Cats are the most popular pets in the United States and in many other countries as well. There are some 58 million pet cats in the United States, and they outnumber dogs (the longtime holder of the number-one spot) by 6 million.

What is the reason for the cat's great popularity? Much of it has to do with today's lifestyle. With more people living in city apartments, cats have become the pet of choice because of their convenience. They are small, quiet, and don't need to be taken out for a walk. Also, with both parents working in so many households, cats make an easy-to-care-for pet.

Although huge numbers of people provide wonderful homes for their pet cats, there are also millions of unwanted cats and kittens with no homes at all. Many of these homeless cats become wild and are killed by other animals, by cars, or by people. And over 5 million must be put to death every year at animal-control centers all over the country.

If more owners accepted responsibility for their cats and had them neutered, the homeless cat population could be greatly reduced. A female cat that is not spayed and is wandering on her

own will have litter after litter of kittens. In fact, she can have as many as one hundred kittens over an eight-year period. If you multiply this by the millions of stray female cats, you'll quickly see the problem.

Becoming Your Cat's Best Friend is a book for young cat owners. It will give you a better understanding of your cat and why it acts the way it does. By learning more about your cat, you can learn to be a better cat owner. That way, you can give your cat a long, happy, and secure life. In turn, your cat will give you love and countless hours of enjoyment.

WHERE DID MY CAT COME FROM?

The cat family, called Felidae, ranges from the small house cat to the Siberian tiger, which can weigh up to 600 pounds (272 kilograms). All are from the Carnivora order, which means that they are meat-eating mammals. And all cats, from the tabby to the tiger, have agile low-slung bodies, small finely formed heads, and long tails to aid in balance. They also have specialized teeth and claws that are used for hunting.

The first wild cats are thought to have appeared some 10 million years ago. The basic characteristics of the cat family have changed amazingly little during that time, although the animals evolved into many sizes and colorations over the years.

The domestic cat (*Felis catus*) can be traced back 5,000 years to ancient Egypt. The Egyptians domesticated the African wildcat, and this animal is thought to be the ancestor of today's house cats. The African wildcat had "tabby," or striped, markings. These markings are so common in our house cats that tabby has become another word for cat.

The taming of the African wildcat started when it began hunting the rodents (rats and mice) that infested the farms and grain storehouses of the Egyptians. Over time the cats became tame, and people began taking them into their homes as both mousers and pets.

By about 1500 B.C. (nearly 3,500 years ago), the Egyptians began to worship the cat as a sacred animal. They had a cat goddess named Bast, who had the head of a cat and the body of a woman. When a pet cat died, the household went into mourning. The cat was made into a mummy and buried in a special cat cemetery.

THIS IS MORE LIKE IT!

About 1000 B.C., Egyptian cats were brought to Italy by Phoenician and Greek traders. Over many centuries, cats gradually spread throughout Europe, arriving in England by about A.D. 900.

Cats were brought to America as mousers by the earliest settlers in the 1600s—they were most likely aboard the *Mayflower* in 1620. Most of the cats in the United States today are descendants of these colonial cats.

As the domestic cat spread to nearly all corners of the globe, more selective breeding began. That's why there are many breeds of cats today, much like there are breeds of dogs.

Some big cats, such as the Asiatic lion, the tiger, cheetah, and leopard, are having trouble surviving in the wild. Many are being killed, and the places in which they live (their habitats) are disappearing.

Domestic cats, however, are thriving. There are more cat owners than ever but, unfortunately, more unwanted cats as well. If you love cats, learning all you can about them can make a difference.

TYPES OF CATS

There are about thirty breeds of cats, which are divided into two basic categories: shorthairs and longhairs. The American shorthair and the Siamese are two of the best-known shorthaired cats. The Persian is the most popular longhaired cat.

Many cat lovers will become attached to a particular breed, such as a Himalayan (a cross between the Persian and the Siamese), and they will choose only that kind as a pet. But some purebred cats can be very expensive.

If you are looking for a family pet and are not interested in showing or breeding it, the common house cat can be just as satisfying as a purebred. You can most likely get a kitten free of charge because so many unwanted litters are born every day. Check the advertisements in the newspaper or visit your local humane society for kittens that are up for adoption.

But whether you buy or adopt, your pet will probably weigh between 6 and 10 pounds (2.7 and 4.5 kilograms) when fully grown. Occasionally, a cat may grow to weigh 15 pounds (10 kilograms) or more.

A cat's life span is a little longer than a dog's. Cats that are kept in the house and watched carefully outside can live about fifteen to seventeen years. Some even live to nineteen or twenty. Cats allowed to wander on their own will almost certainly have a much shorter life span. These animals are more likely to get into fights, be exposed to rain and snow, eat poorly, and generally lead a less healthy life.

Unlike dogs, where the breeds can vary quite a bit in size and temperament, most cats are similar to each other, although there are some general differences among breeds. A good book on the various breeds will describe each.

CAT OR KITTEN

If you are choosing a kitten as your pet, it should be one that already has had a good deal of contact with people during its first two months of life. The kitten should appear healthy and lively, and have been kept in a clean environment.

The choice of male or female is up to the buyer. But most cats should eventually be neutered unless you have a specific reason to breed. When neutered, males and females are equally affectionate and loving. A spayed female will be more likely to accept a new kitten or cat in the home. The behavior problems of unneutered cats are explained later in this book.

If your family decides to adopt an adult cat, try to find one with a known personality. Has it lived inside a home before?

Does it use a litter box? Is it affectionate, or has it been mistreated or neglected? Has it been neutered? Unless you or a member of your family is experienced with cats, you may find some behaviors that are difficult to handle.

Be careful adopting stray cats that wander into your life. If a stray cat seems to choose your family or home as its own, make sure to take it to a veterinarian as quickly as possible for a thorough checkup and vaccinations.

Most cats want a safe and secure home. But kittens that are born outside and have absolutely no contact with humans during their first two or three months of life will become wild, or feral. These unfortunate animals may find it difficult to change their ways and adapt to a new kind of life.

WHAT CAN I EXPECT FROM MY CAT?

One day you are happily surprised when your parents decide to add a family pet to the household. But you live in an apartment, and both your parents work. They say that you can't have a dog because it will make too much noise and will have to be walked all the time. They don't even want a pet bird because birds sometimes screech and throw food around their cage.

Then someone suggests getting a cat. They're clean, quiet, and can be left alone most of the time. They use a litter box and don't have to be walked. They are playful as kittens, but when they grow up you hardly know they are there. A perfect apartment pet.

A few days later, Kitty comes home. Sure, the new kitten is cute and playful. But Mom didn't expect those scratches on the legs of her antique table. And Dad didn't expect to have the plant knocked off his desk and his newspaper shredded. You are annoyed by the way the kitten "attacks" your pants leg whenever you walk by.

Two weeks later your parents say they made a mistake. One day when you come home from school, Kitty is gone. Your parents decide to get some fish instead.

This kind of unfortunate situation can happen when people don't have enough information about the pet they are getting.

Let's look at the way nature has designed cats to be the expert hunters they are, as well as how cats live in their natural environment. By knowing how cats live in the wild, you'll be able to understand why your pet sometimes acts the way it does.

CAT CHARACTERISTICS

Because their ancestors were hunters, cats have highly developed abilities to hunt and to defend themselves. A cat's claws are long, curved, and sharper than those of any other mammal. Unlike other animals, cats' claws are retractable: They are hidden inside sheaths on top of each toe. A cat can extend or pull in its claws whenever it wants.

Claws are used for grasping during the hunt, for defense, and for climbing. The claws are so strong that a cat could even cling to a cement wall if it had the proper toeholds.

A cat's skin contains very few sweat glands. It cleans itself by sloughing off old skin and hair. That way, the cat gives off little odor for its enemies in the wild to detect. This also helps make the house cat a pleasant animal to have around. But because the cat doesn't perspire much, it should never be left in a place where it can become overheated, especially in a car.

All of a cat's five senses (sight, sound, smell, taste, and touch) are well developed, some more so than others. A cat's eyes can detect the slightest movement from great distances and can see in light that is six times dimmer than people can. Again, this is important to a cat's survival in the wild.

A cat's ears are constantly moving to pick up the faintest sounds that will tell it of impending danger. A cat's hearing is five times more acute than ours and three times better than a dog's.

Cats hear high-pitched sounds especially well. They can detect the scratches and squeals made by mice and rats in their holes. Because of their sensitive hearing, cats dislike and fear loud noises. You'll probably see your cat take off as soon as the vacuum cleaner is turned on.

Cats also have an amazing sense of touch. They often use their noses and the pads of the front feet. And each hair on their body is very sensitive. This is why cats love to have their body stroked.

Whiskers are also part of the cat's sense of touch. They grow in four rows on what is considered the upper lip of the cat. They also grow on the cheeks, over the eyes, and even on the front legs. Whiskers act like antennae for the cat, helping to guide it through rocky terrain and thick underbrush while hunting at night. Whiskers are also thought to pick up vibrations in the air to warn the animal about abrupt changes in the weather.

BASIC INSTINCTS

In the wild, the cat is basically a solitary animal. It lives alone and hunts alone. Some kinds of cats (such as lions) do live together, but in a loose grouping with no leader. This is why the domestic cat tends to be independent and prefers to do things on its own.

This does not mean that pet cats are antisocial, however. Cats in the same household can become very attached to each other, sharing the same bed and grooming each other with loving care. Cats also display affection toward their owners, wanting to be in close contact with them, preferably on their laps.

Being solitary animals, each cat in the wild claims its own territory, or range. Territory is of utmost importance to cats and determines much of their behavior. A cat marks the objects in the area it claims by spraying urine, scratching, or rubbing up against them. (Cats have special scent glands on their heads and at the base of their tails. By rubbing against an object they leave their scent.)

Like their wild cousins, house cats have a need to "own" property. When you take in a cat, your home becomes its territory. To stake its claim, the cat will scratch and rub up against objects in the house. Since you are included in the territory, the cat will rub back and forth against your leg. Unneutered cats will also spray urine.

The cat's homing instinct is a striking example of how attached it gets to its territory. After a family moves, cats have been known to run away from their new home in search of their old one. Incredibly, some cats do find their way back to their old hunting grounds. But more often than not, this ends very unhappily, with the cat never being found again.

If you move, therefore, plan to keep your cat inside the new house for about a week. Once it gets used to its new surroundings, it will start to think of them as its territory. Also, if you take your cat on vacations, make sure to keep it in a carrier (or on a leash if it's trained to one) when outside.

IS IT EASY TO CARE FOR MY PET?

If you know a few basic rules and follow some simple guidelines, it is relatively easy to care for your cat. Remember, although cats like to give the impression that they are self-sufficient, your pet will depend on you for its care.

FOOD

Over the past several decades, the pet-food industry has made tremendous strides. Pet foods are now scientifically developed. This makes feeding your pet an easy job. But you must still take special care to follow some rules.

When cats in the wild kill prey, they don't feed only on the meat. First, they will eat the stomach contents, assuring themselves of some partially digested greens. Then they eat the meat. Their instincts give them a naturally balanced diet.

That's why you cannot simply feed your cat canned tuna, chicken, and table scraps. That won't give the cat a balanced diet and will eventually lead to health problems. Use a commercial cat food and always look for food that is labeled "complete and balanced." This means that it has been tested and certified as a nutritionally sound diet.

If you decide to change your cat's diet (from canned to semi-moist, for example), be patient. It's best to make the change gradually, replacing the old food with the new over the course of a week. Cats like what is familiar and resist change. Your cat may be stubborn and refuse to eat for a day or two. But once it gets hungry enough, it will adjust to the change.

Cats should be fed at a set time each day. Two meals for adult cats—morning and evening—are fine. (Kittens should be fed more often.) Also, it's important to always have a bowl of fresh water available to your cat.

Do not feed it anything that contains bones, such as fish or chicken. A sharp bone can easily become stuck in a cat's throat

and choke it. Don't feed your cat any large chunks of food. Unlike humans and dogs, cats cannot grind food. Their jaws do not move sideways, only up and down. A cat will swallow food as soon as it's small enough to go down the throat.

FAT CATS

No one wants to have a fat cat, but if you're not careful, your cat will overeat and gain weight. Once again, part of the reason is a leftover instinct from the wild. In the wild, finding food occupies a major part of most animals' lives.

Many experts believe that a cat is always thinking about food. If it catches the odor of something it likes, then it wants to eat. For your cat's sake, however, don't give in and feed it too much. An overweight cat is more likely to have health problems and will not live as long as a cat that is slim and trim.

HOW ABOUT EXERCISE?

Your cat is a natural-born athlete that can run, jump, and climb with great speed and agility. Just as a lion or tiger will become depressed in a small cage, a house cat won't be happy confined to a small area with no chance to exercise. Exercise is a must for good health and muscle tone.

If you neglect your indoor cat, it may exercise on its own and do a great deal of damage to the house. Cats have been

known to try to climb curtains, jump onto tables and knock valuable items to the floor, and scratch on furniture.

It's best to provide your cat with a number of toys and to set aside a special playtime of at least fifteen minutes a day. Just use your cat's natural instincts. For example, cats love to chase and pounce. You can use something like a tennis or Ping-Pong ball, or a stuffed toy. Make sure not to use your fingers as a toy with a kitten, so it won't get into the bad habit of biting or scratching people's hands.

Between play sessions, your cat will find ways to entertain itself. Batting a pencil across the floor, watching water drip from a faucet, and sitting on the windowsill to spy on birds at the feeder are just a few of their amusements.

DOWNTIME

Your cat won't spend the whole day working out at the gym, however. A great deal of its time is reserved for the all-important catnap. In fact, cats are the biggest sleepers of all mammals. They sleep from sixteen to eighteen hours out of twenty-four. Most of the cat's sleep (some 70 percent) is in the light sleep of the catnap: The rest is deep sleep.

Every cat should have a warm, comfortable bed. A commercial cat bed, an old chair, or a basket or box works well inside. The bed should not be in an area of heavy household traffic, and it should not be in a place where there are cold drafts.

Cats are nocturnal, meaning that they are active at night. In the wild, cats set out to catch prey at nightfall. This is why kit-

YAWN.
I'VE BEEN UP FOR ALMOST AN HOUR!
TIME FOR A NAP!

tens often have a burst of activity at the end of the day some people call the "evening crazies." This is also why your cat likes to prowl around the house in the middle of the night.

THE LITTER BOX

The litter box is an important piece of equipment for all owners of indoor cats. It should be kept as far away from the cat's food and water as possible. Many cats will simply refuse to relieve themselves close to where they eat.

Fill the box with at least 2 inches (5 centimeters) of a commercial kitty litter. This will be enough to absorb urine and allow the cat to cover its feces. If you don't use enough litter, the cat may refuse to use the box.

In the wild, all cats dig holes to cover their droppings, so training is not difficult. A new cat may have to be confined for a very short time in the room with the litter box. You may also take a kitten to the box, pick up its paws, and make a scratching motion. In this way, you are appealing to the cat's natural instincts.

NEAT AND TIDY

Cats are naturally clean animals, so grooming the shorthaired breeds is relatively easy. Shorthairs can be brushed or combed once a week. Longhaired breeds should be groomed every day with a special brush. They should be brushed against the grain (toward the head), with special care taken when the animal is shedding heavily, especially in the springtime.

Cats often groom themselves by licking and can swallow a huge amount of hair if not brushed enough. This hair can cause furballs to form in the cat's stomach. Furballs cause vomiting and sometimes serious constipation. Regular brushing can help prevent furballs from forming.

If you let your cat outside, make sure that you attach a collar with a name tag. The collar should have a special elastic section so that if it catches on something, the cat won't be choked. Never put a ribbon around the neck of a cat or kitten. It looks cute but could choke the cat.

THE DILEMMA OF SCRATCHING

There is no way to stop a cat from using its claws to scratch. Aside from marking territory by scratching, the cat scratches to sharpen its claws. In the wild, the cat's claws are a major part of its defense and survival, so the animal has a strong instinct to keep the claws in tip-top shape.

Scratching can be very damaging to your furniture, carpets, and drapes. Since no kind of punishment or training will keep a cat from scratching, you must make sure that it scratches where it won't cause damage. The best way to do this is to set up a scratching post when the kitten or cat comes into the home.

The scratching post should be 3 to 4 four feet (about 1 to 2 meters) high and 8 to 12 inches (20 to 30 centimeters) in diameter. In this way the post will be tall enough for the cat to stretch out full length while scratching, which gives it good exercise. The post needs to have a sturdy base so that it does not move while the cat is scratching. This could frighten the cat.

Natural bark, which can be a sawed-off tree limb, makes an excellent scratching post. Pet stores also carry a variety of ready-made, carpet-covered posts.

Place the post near the cat's bed because the first thing that a cat does after getting up is to stretch and sharpen its claws. If the post is attractive and easily available, your cat will use it from the beginning.

Sometimes a cat doesn't take to its scratching post, preferring instead the edge of the hall rug or a wicker chair. In this case

it may be a good idea to keep the cat's claws trimmed so that its scratching is less destructive. Only the very tip of the claw, which is white, should be clipped. Have your vet show you the correct way to do this.

If these measures fail, owners sometimes resort to having the cat's claws surgically removed. If the front paws are declawed, the cat can go through the scratching motions but won't do any damage. A new kitten cannot be declawed immediately. This could cause growth problems in the feet. Some experts say to wait at least three months; others suggest six.

Declawing is permanent—the claws will never grow back. Once the cat has been declawed it must always be kept inside, because a declawed cat cannot defend itself or climb a tree to escape danger.

Experts do not agree on the subject of declawing. Some feel that declawing usually has no bad side effects and that declawed cats are perfectly fine. Other experts, however, believe that declawing can harm the cat physically and psychologically. They say that it upsets the cat's balance and may make it become anxious and unfriendly. It could also make the cat more likely to bite since it no longer has its first line of defense, its claws. Consult a vet you trust for advice.

"HERE KITTY, KITTY"

It's up to you to train your cat to be a well-behaved pet that follows the house rules. A firm "No!" is the word that you should use when you want to stop your cat from doing something wrong: when it jumps up on furniture, when it scratches your favorite chair, when it tries to steal food from the kitchen table.

At the same time you say "No!" move the cat firmly but gently from the scene of the crime. When you pick your cat up, make sure to support it under the chest and hind legs. Never pick it up by the scruff of the neck—only the mother cat is allowed to do this.

In addition, you must never hit your cat. In the wild, cats are not programmed to submit to a leader. Your cat will either shy away from you or get angry if you hit it. And you may lose its trust. When the cat behaves, praise it and pet it. You can even give it a little treat.

If your cat is still misbehaving, however, some trainers will throw something near (*never* at) the cat as they say "No!" It may be a set of noisy keys or a magazine. Other trainers recommend squirting the cat with water from a water pistol or plant sprayer.

Your cat should also learn its name. Use its name to call it to dinner or to praise it. But don't use its name when you are scolding it. It should associate only pleasant things with its name.

This is as far as most owners go in training their cats. Cats can also be trained to walk on a leash and to obey commands such as come, sit, and stop. If you decide you want to do this with your cat, there are good books on training. Or you can find a professional cat trainer to help you. Most owners, however, are happy with their free-spirited cats as long as they observe the house rules.

SAFETY FIRST

Cats, and especially kittens, need to be protected from various household hazards. Kitty-proofing your house will help prevent unfortunate accidents. This should be done before you bring your pet home.

Make sure all windows have secure screens. Household cleansers and other chemical products should be put out of reach, as should small objects your pet could swallow, such as nails, tacks, rubber bands, string, thread, and yarn.

Many cats like to nibble on houseplants, but some types are poisonous, including dieffenbachia (dumb cane), philodendron, poinsettia, and English ivy. Put all these out of reach of your cat. Or, better yet, replace them with nonpoisonous plants, such as Swedish ivy, African violets, spider plants, ferns, and palms. Note also that the berries of bittersweet, Christmas cherry, holly, and mistletoe are deadly to cats.

Kittens like to explore every nook and cranny of your house and may get trapped by mistake. Keep this in mind before closing an open dresser drawer or a kitchen cabinet. Cats also like to nap in warm clothes dryers, so make sure to always shut the dryer door. Also, keep oven, refrigerator, and freezer doors closed.

Aside from the obvious dangers of speeding cars and other animals, your cat will also encounter hazards in its own backyard. Especially dangerous are chemicals stored in garages and sheds (antifreeze and pesticides). There are also many poisonous outdoor plants, such as daffodils, azaleas, and laurels, to name a few.

In addition, some outdoor cats like to crawl up into the engine compartment of parked cars to take a snooze on a still-warm engine. Be sure to bang on the hood or beep the horn before anyone starts the car.

I DIDN'T KNOW THESE THINGS ABOUT MY CAT

As you have already seen, many of the things your cat will do in your home come from instincts learned over thousands of years of living in the wild. Here are some other important considerations for cat owners.

ADDING ANOTHER CAT

You love your cat, but find you are spending less and less time with it. Your parents are at work, and you are spending a lot of time at school and with your friends. You are worried (and rightly so) that your cat is lonely. Your family decides to get a second cat. That way, the cats will have each other when no one else is home.

Many cat owners make this decision. But before adding to your household, there are some things you must know about a cat's behavior. For starters, adult cats can be very territorial, and they will defend that territory if they think someone is intruding upon it.

The best way to avoid potentially dangerous cat fights is to raise a pair of kittens together. If you have an adult cat, it's best to bring a kitten home as a second cat instead of another adult. And a cat of the opposite sex has a better chance of being accepted than one of the same sex.

When adding a second cat to the household, be sure to supervise all the early meetings between the two animals. Don't force them to be together or to like each other right away. If they are allowed to get to know each other on their own terms, it will work out much better. It's also important to give both cats extra love and reassurance.

If the two cats fight at first, feed them separately and let them sleep in different rooms. In a week or so they should have worked out a satisfactory relationship.

OTHER KINDS OF PETS

Because the cat is a natural hunter, a normally quiet house cat may spring into action once it realizes there is a small animal in the house. Birds, hamsters, and fish are all potential victims when a cat is in the same home.

Try to make bird and hamster cages as secure as possible. Then put them in a place that the cat will have trouble reaching. Cover all fish tanks with a solid hood. House cats have defeated many security measures while left alone. When you aren't home, try to separate the cat from any small animals.

Cats and dogs have been known to live together peacefully and even be friends. This is most likely to occur if the animals were raised together as puppy and kitten. If you bring one into a home where the other already lives, there can be big problems. The animal that was there first will most likely be jealous and won't like having its territory invaded. Again, great care must be taken if this is to work.

WHAT DO THESE SOUNDS MEAN?

Cats express themselves with a variety of distinctive sounds. Here's what some of them mean.

Purring—Purring is a low, vibrating sound that almost sounds like a growl. You may feel your cat purr as it sits on your lap. This is a sign that your cat is relaxed and contented. Sometimes, however, purring can also show nervousness or pain.

The interesting thing is that purring doesn't come from the vocal cords. It is thought that the sound comes from a vibration of blood vessels in the chest area. This is one of the real mystery sounds of the animal world.

Meowing—Everyone is familiar with a cat's meow. Sometimes it's cute. You feel that your cat is talking to you. Sometimes it can be long and grating, a kind of crying. The meow may be thought of as mainly an attention-getting sound.

Kittens may begin meowing because they are small and alone and new in your house. They want attention, much like a baby does when it cries. When you comfort the kitten, it has what it wants. After that, meowing can be a way for the cat to get things from you—food, toys, attention, to be let into a room, and so forth.

Meowing can become a bad habit. A firm "No!" will sometimes help curtail it. But with some cats, especially Siamese, plan to listen to a good deal of meowing.

Hissing—This sound is an unmistakable warning. Watch out. A hissing cat is not a happy one. In fact, it is hissing out of fear or anger. If you come upon a cat that is hissing and also has an arched back or bushy tail, don't go any closer. It may attack you!

Growling—How many movies have you seen with big cats like lions and tigers giving off a deep, frightening growl. Your cat

can growl, too. But house cats don't growl often. Growling is usually done by a mother cat who is protecting her kittens. It's a deep growl from down in the throat. It can sound very threatening, which is just what it's meant to be.

BODY LANGUAGE

Sounds are just a part of the entire picture. Your cat will talk to you in many other ways. You'll also have to learn your cat's body language—how it moves its tail, ears, paws, and entire body.

Cats will tell their owners how they are feeling in the same way they will tell other cats. So the body language that your cat uses with you comes from thousands of years in the wild and being with other cats as well as other animals.

When a cat carries its tail high, it is usually happy and content. By contrast, a tail that's held low, or drooped down, indicates an unhappy cat and one that might be best left alone. If the tail is twitching or lashing back and forth, it might be best to watch out. The cat may be angry and getting ready to attack. As a rule, the faster the twitch or a twitch turning to a lash, the angrier the cat is becoming.

Ears alert and standing straight up indicate a good mood. A cat at play will hold its ears this way. By contrast, ears pulled downward means that the cat is becoming defensive about something happening around it. Ears downward and pulled to the rear indicate an angry cat. This position will probably go hand-in-hand with a twitching tail.

When a cat reaches out its paw without claws showing, it is making a friendly—even affectionate—gesture. Your cat may wake you up every morning with a gentle tap of the paw on your cheek. This is its way of saying good morning to you—and reminding you that kitty needs breakfast. An extended paw with claws showing is quite another matter. It is clearly a warning sign.

When the cat is creeping slowly, crouched low with its belly close to the ground, it is stalking, ready to pounce on real or suspected prey. This movement is also used in certain kinds of play. A cat on its back with its belly up is also showing that it is in the mood to play.

WHY IS MY CAT DOING THAT?

Why is my cat making a strange face as if it just ate something awful?
Why does my cat kill mice and then bring them to me?
Why do my cat's eyes glow in the dark?
Is it dangerous to have my cat around my new baby brother?

Questions such as these are often asked by new cat owners. These reflect characteristics and behaviors that are part of a cat's ancestry. They are things that a cat does by instinct, and will probably always do. The more you understand about these and other behaviors, the more you will understand your cat. Let's take a look at some of the behaviors that your cat will most likely bring into your home.

You may sometimes notice your cat making a strange face. Its mouth is slightly open, its nose wrinkled, and its upper lip curled back. This has been described as a "grimace of disgust," as if the animal has just smelled or tasted something awful. But it's not really that. Cats, as well as some other animals, have an unusual sense organ located in the roof of the mouth just behind the front teeth. Called Jacobson's organ, it is a tiny pouch with tubes that open into the mouth and nose.

45

This organ gives the cat a special sense that is a combination of taste and smell. When your cat makes that funny face, it is actually pressing its tongue against the opening in the mouth that leads to Jacobson's organ. What it is doing is testing an odor of food or something in the air by using this special organ. (Interestingly, humans used to have a functioning Jacobson's organ, but like the appendix it is no longer in use.)

Many people are puzzled and often disgusted by this next cat behavior. In fact, they often misunderstand the reason for it. You might be sitting in your room doing homework or watching television, and your cat will enter the room with something in its mouth. Without warning, it will drop a dead mouse or other small animal at your feet.

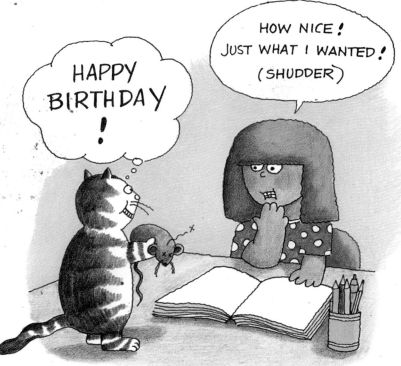

Many people wonder why the cat doesn't eat its prey. To understand exactly what the cat is doing, we must once again look at its wild cousins: They are known to bring their prey to other cats as a social gesture. So your cat is simply bringing you a present! It is the cat's way of doing something for its person. Since this is a love offering, don't yell at your cat or punish it. Simply dispose of the dead animal and accept the reason your cat brought it to you.

If you shine a flashlight in a dark room and your cat is in the vicinity, you'll catch the remarkable glow of its eyes. This is called "eyeshine," and it has a golden or greenish color in most cats. In Siamese, however, the glow is red.

Eyeshine is caused by a special membrane, or layer, at the back of the cat's eyes. Called the tapetum lucidum, it is made of layers of sparkling cells. This membrane acts like a mirror, reflecting light and helping the cat see better in near darkness.

With the help of the tapetum lucidum, the cat can see well enough to hunt on a starlit night even if the moon is not out. And inside your house, your cat can see in a darkened room even when you can no longer see your hand in front of your face.

There is an old wives' tale that cats would sometimes suck a baby's breath and possibly kill the child. This is absolutely not true. But certain instinctive behaviors make it necessary to watch cats around newborn babies.

A cat looking for a warm, comfortable place to sleep can sometimes curl up next to a sleeping baby's face. Smothering then becomes a possibility. And a cat sleeping in a corner of a baby's crib might decide that spot is part of its territory. If the baby rolls or flails its arms or legs into the cat's spot, the instinct to protect territory might make the cat strike out with its paws and give the baby a bad scratch.

Some young cats, when sitting on your lap, will begin to paw and scratch at your knees and thighs. This can be a painful habit, with the cat's claws causing rips in clothing and scratches on your skin. But this also is an instinctual behavior.

This kind of pawing is called kneading. Kittens will often paw their mother's body in a similar way as they nurse. Then it's a sign of contentment and also encourages milk production in the mother. Young cats weaned from their mothers too soon will often knead when on your lap.

The kneading habit can sometimes be stopped by putting newspaper or aluminum foil on your lap. (Make sure, however, that your cat doesn't eat any of the foil.) The cat won't get the same feeling from the newspaper or foil and will often stop kneading after awhile. It is also good to keep the cat's claws trimmed so that if it does knead, it won't be so uncomfortable for you.

Behaviors and instincts from the wild still dominate much of your cat's life. The more you understand about these instincts and how they still appear in a full-time house cat, the more you can work with your cat. And by doing that, you will have a better and happier pet.

WHAT'S WRONG
WITH MY CAT?

With good care, a balanced diet, enough exercise, and attention, your cat should be a vigorous, happy, and healthy animal for many years. Other precautions should be taken to keep a cat healthy. Find a veterinarian you like and trust, and take your cat for checkups once a year. Make sure your cat has all the recommended vaccinations for rabies, feline distemper, feline leukemia, and other cat diseases. Many of these require a yearly booster shot.

You must also, however, watch for signs of illness between visits to the vet. You should observe your cat every day. If it has a good appetite and suddenly stops eating, something is wrong. If its coat loses its usually sleek and glossy look, watch carefully.

A cat that is not feeling well will stop grooming itself. That alone will cause the coat to look rough, dull, and scruffy. So if the look and feel of the coat changes, the red flag should go up: It's time to see the vet.

You can also give your cat a quick checkup as it sits contentedly on your lap. While you are petting the cat you can check its coat, skin, ears, teeth, and gums. If anything seems out of the ordinary, call your vet.

In checking your cat, the two most common problems you are likely to find are fleas and ear mites. You may spot the fleas themselves or else their droppings, which are small dark particles frequently found at the base of the cat's tail. Ears that have dark waxy dirt in them can be a sign of mites. If you see anything like this on your cat, call your vet.

Be sure that you give your cat only the medication prescribed by your vet. Some of our medications, such as aspirin and Tylenol, can be harmful or even deadly to your cat.

THE IMPORTANCE OF SPAYING AND NEUTERING

Cat owners should seriously consider having their pet cat spayed or neutered for several very important reasons. An unspayed female cat (called a queen) and an unneutered male cat (called a tom) are much like other animals—their instinct is to breed, and this can lead to several undesirable behaviors.

When the female is in heat, or receptive to breeding, she may cry or wail for hours on end, day and night, for a week or more. There is no training that can stop or change this natural behavior.

Male cats, when sexually mature (starting at about six to eight months), will often mark their territories by spraying strong-smelling urine on the walls and furniture. The male is warning other male cats to keep away. If he senses a female in heat he may also run around the house, often howling and keeping his owners up all night.

Male and female cats that have not been altered and are left outside will give their owners still other problems. Males will get into vicious fights over available females. And your female cat may well give you something you aren't prepared to handle—a litter of unwanted kittens.

Spaying and neutering are relatively simple operations from which cats recover quickly. Once the surgery is done, you will have a happier, healthier pet. Most altered cats are more affectionate toward their owners and more content with their lives. They are also less likely to get certain illnesses, such as breast tumors, later in life.

THE OLDER CAT

In their natural habitat in the wild, not many animals reach old age. Fortunately, our house cats can live comfortably for many years. Most cats don't start to show their age until the early to mid-teens. You'll know it when it happens.

You may first notice that your cat is sleeping more. It may not want to play with that Ping-Pong ball as much. It may not jump up on your bed with the same spring. It may not run and dart around the room without warning, just to get some exercise. Instead, it prefers to curl up in its warm bed and watch the world go by.

When this happens, it's time to pay even more attention to your longtime friend. Your aging cat needs you more than ever. Not only do you have to keep an older cat comfortable, but you have to watch its health more closely.

Older cats love affection. Yet they may not come to you as often as they used to. It's sometimes easy to forget that they are there. Make sure you give your older cat affection as much as or more than before. It will love being stroked, hearing your voice reassure it, and just knowing you are there.

NYAH NYAH!

NYAH!

If your pet is an only cat, this may not be the right time to bring a kitten into the house. The kitten will want to play when the old cat wants to sleep. It is sometimes a bad combination. The old cat will be stressed by the kitten, and it still has the potential to hurt the younger animal.

With an older cat, be alert for everything. Don't let your cat become overweight. Watch for changes in litter-box habits. If it suddenly stops using the litter box or urinates all over the house, it may have a bladder or kidney problem. If it starts drinking a lot more water than usual, this may also be a sign of a kidney problem.

A cat that is having trouble moving or jumping may have a touch of arthritis and need medication from the vet. A dry and shedding coat can lead to more and bigger furballs. More brushing may be necessary, especially since older cats don't always attend to their grooming needs as well as they used to.

Veterinary medicine has made huge strides when it comes to taking care of older animals. Special diets and medications that help your pet live longer and be more comfortable are available. Vet checks at least twice a year are also a good idea.

When your pet is no longer happy and comfortable, it may be time to say good-bye. Your vet will help you with the decision. Euthanasia is a word from the Greek meaning gentle and easy death. When the time has come, your vet will give your animal a painless injection that is an overdose of an anesthetic. Your cat will lose consciousness almost immediately. As hard as this is to go through, it is the final show of love and kindness you can give your old friend.

WHAT IF WE HAVE KITTENS?

There are two kinds of pregnancies in female cats—the planned and the unplanned. In theory, there should never be an unplanned pregnancy. To make sure there is never an accident, have your female cat spayed. End of story. But if your pet female cat is going to have kittens, whether planned or unplanned, there are some things you should know.

It is difficult to tell if a female cat is pregnant until about four weeks after she has mated with a male. You may notice that the female's nipples take on a pink color and become slightly enlarged. But your vet can tell for sure by palpating, or feeling, your cat's abdomen. The vet can feel the tiny kittens within the uterus. Do not try to examine your cat's abdomen yourself. It could cause damage to your cat and the developing kittens.

After five weeks, you'll notice the pregnant cat's abdomen becoming slightly pear-shaped and beginning to swell. The kittens will be born about 65 days from mating. The average litter consists of four kittens.

Female cats should be treated as usual during pregnancy. Carrying kittens and giving birth is a completely natural and instinctive behavior. Unless there is an obvious problem, your

cat's life should not change much during pregnancy. It will be careful on its own, especially in running and jumping and in squeezing through small openings.

You may have to feed your cat several smaller meals, because she cannot take in as much food at one time during the later stages of pregnancy. And don't let her gain too much weight. You should try to give your cat exercise without forcing her. Several vet checks during the pregnancy are also a good idea.

By the seventh week, your cat will begin to look for a place to nest. You should provide a large shallow box with comfortable bedding in a quiet, warm, dark corner. A full carton with a top can also be used, with a hole cut in the side as an entrance. The hole should be chest-high to the mother cat. Place a thick layer of newspapers over the bedding. Mother cat will scratch at the newspapers and shift them around. This is part of its natural instinct, fixing up a nest.

Mother cats know just what to do when the kittens are born. You can ask your vet what to look for, and be sure an adult is around once the cat is ready to give birth. If you see anything that doesn't look right or if the mother seems to be struggling to have the kittens, call the vet immediately.

Kittens are blind and deaf for the first seven to ten days. But their sense of smell keeps them close to their mother and leads them to the nipples, where they can drink her milk. Eyes begin opening in a week or so, and the kittens begin to hear sounds at two weeks. Baby, or milk, teeth begin to come out about this

time. When the kittens are about four weeks old, mother cat will begin to wean (stop nursing) them. Now it's time to start handling the kittens and gently playing with them so they will get used to people.

By the time they are eight weeks old, the kittens should be weaned enough to stop taking milk from the mother. From this point on they will be ready to go to new homes.

GOOD HOMES ARE MOST IMPORTANT

Because there are so many unwanted cats, placing kittens is very important. If you planned your breeding, you probably already have homes for the kittens. But if you had an unplanned litter, you'll have to make a special effort to find good homes.

Remember, these kittens didn't ask to come into the world. They deserve the same kind of good home you give the mother cat. So try to find the best homes available. If you place an ad in the newspaper, don't be afraid to ask questions when people call about the kittens.

Try to find out if the callers know much about cats and their needs. If their homes don't seem satisfactory to you, you don't have to sell or give them a kitten. It is up to you and your family to pick the best homes and give each kitten a chance for a long and happy life.

Cats are valued pet friends that add joy to our lives. Although they have adapted to living in our homes, some of the tiger is still in the tabby. By understanding the basic instincts that your cat carries with it from the wild, you will know why it acts the way it does. And this will help you give your pet the best possible home.

FIND OUT MORE

Arnold, Caroline. *Cats: In From the Wild*. Minneapolis: Lerner, 1993.

Howard, Tom. *The Love of Cats*. New York: Smithmark, 1992.

Jameson, Pam, and Tina Hearne. *Responsible Pet Care Series*. Vero Beach, FL: Rourke Publications, 1989.

McPherson, Mark. *Choosing Your Pet*. Mahwah, NJ: Troll Associates, 1985.

Roach, Margaret J. *I Love You, Charles Henry: Cats and Dogs in My Life*. Corvallis, OR: Maggie Roach & Associates, 1994.

INDEX